Trigger Your ADHD Potential: Transforming ADHD Challenges into Triumphs

Johann Horsley

Strategies for Success in Work, Relationships, and Life

Contents

INTRODUCTION

Welcome to "Trigger Your ADHD Potential: Transforming ADHD Challenges into Triumphs." In this book, we embark on a journey of discovery, empowerment, and transformation. ADHD (Attention-Deficit/Hyperactivity Disorder) is often misunderstood, stigmatized, and seen solely through the lens of its challenges. However, in these pages, we will demystify ADHD, embracing its neurological differences as strengths rather than limitations. Our goal is to equip you with knowledge, strategies, and insights to unlock your full potential, not despite ADHD but because of it.

CHAPTER 1

Understanding ADHD: Demystifying the Neurological Differences

In this chapter, we delve into the intricate workings of ADHD, shedding light on its neurological underpinnings, behavioral manifestations, and the diverse ways it impacts individuals. By gaining a deeper understanding of ADHD, we can reframe our perspectives, dispel myths, and pave the way for a more inclusive and empowering approach to neurodiversity.

What is ADHD?

The neurodevelopmental disease known as ADHD is typified by recurrent patterns of hyperactivity, impulsivity, and inattention that seriously impair day-to-day functioning and quality of life. It affects people of all ages, from children to adults, and manifests in various ways across different individuals.

Neurological Insights

To understand ADHD, we must explore its neurological roots. Research has shown that ADHD is associated with differences in brain structure, neurotransmitter functioning, and neural network connectivity. Key brain regions involved in ADHD include the prefrontal cortex, responsible for executive functions like planning and impulse control, and the basal ganglia, involved in regulating attention and movement.

Types of ADHD

ADHD is not a one-size-fits-all condition. It falls into three primary subtype categories:

1. **Predominantly Inattentive Presentation (ADHD-PI):** Characterized by difficulties sustaining attention, organizing tasks, and following through on instructions.

2. **Predominantly Hyperactive-Impulsive Presentation (ADHD-HI):** Marked by excessive fidgeting, impulsivity, restlessness, and difficulty waiting or taking turns.

3. **Combined Presentation (ADHD-C):** Involves a combination of both inattentive and hyperactive-impulsive symptoms.

Each subtype presents its unique challenges and strengths, shaping the individual's experiences and strategies for coping and thriving.

ADHD Across the Lifespan

While ADHD is often associated with childhood, it persists into adolescence and adulthood for many individuals. The presentation of symptoms may evolve over time, with hyperactivity often decreasing but inattention and impulsivity remaining significant challenges.

Myths and Realities

Unfortunately, ADHD is surrounded by misconceptions and stereotypes. Some common myths include the belief that ADHD is just a lack of discipline or that individuals with ADHD are lazy or unintelligent. In reality, ADHD is a complex neurobiological condition with genetic, environmental, and developmental factors at play. Understanding these realities is crucial for fostering empathy, support, and effective interventions.

Impact on Daily Life

Living with ADHD can affect various aspects of daily life, including academics, work performance, relationships, self-esteem, and mental health. Challenges such as procrastination, forgetfulness, time management difficulties, and impulsivity can lead to frustration and overwhelm if not addressed proactively.

The Strengths of ADHD

Despite its challenges, ADHD is also accompanied by unique strengths and talents. These may include creativity, hyperfocus on areas of interest, resilience in the face of adversity, and a knack for thinking outside the box. By recognizing and harnessing these strengths, individuals with ADHD can excel in diverse fields and contribute valuable perspectives to society.

Conclusion

In this chapter, we've scratched the surface of understanding ADHD's complexity, from its neurological roots to its impact on daily life. Our journey continues as we delve deeper into strategies for harnessing ADHD's strengths, overcoming obstacles, and unlocking your full potential. Remember, ADHD is not a limitation but a unique way of experiencing the world—a perspective that can lead to remarkable achievements and personal growth.

CHAPTER 2

Embracing Neurodiversity: The Power of ADHD in a Diverse World

Neurodiversity is a concept that celebrates the natural variations in human brains and cognitive styles. It recognizes that differences in neurology, including conditions like ADHD, autism, dyslexia, and others, are a normal part of the human experience. In this chapter, we explore the concept of neurodiversity and how embracing it can lead to a more inclusive, innovative, and empowered world.

Understanding Neurodiversity

Neurodiversity emphasizes the idea that neurological differences are not inherently good or bad but simply different ways of processing information, thinking, and experiencing the world. It rejects the notion of a neurotypical "normal" and instead promotes acceptance and appreciation of diverse cognitive profiles.

The Spectrum of Neurodiversity

Neurodiversity encompasses a broad spectrum of neurological variations. This spectrum includes conditions such as ADHD, autism spectrum disorder (ASD), dyslexia, dyspraxia, Tourette syndrome, and more. Each condition brings its unique strengths, challenges, and perspectives to the table.

Benefits of Neurodiversity

There are several advantages to accepting neurodiversity for people, groups, and society at large:

1. **Innovation and Creativity:** Neurodivergent individuals often possess unique ways of thinking and problem-solving, leading to innovative ideas and creative solutions.

2. **Diverse Perspectives:** Neurodiversity fosters a range of perspectives and insights, enriching discussions, collaborations, and decision-making processes.

3. **Empathy and Understanding:** Embracing neurodiversity promotes empathy, understanding, and acceptance of differences, creating more inclusive environments.

4. **Neurodiverse Talent Pool:** Organizations that value neurodiversity can tap into a diverse talent pool and benefit from the unique skills and abilities of neurodivergent individuals.

5. **Reduced Stigma:** By challenging stereotypes and promoting acceptance, neurodiversity initiatives contribute to reducing stigma and discrimination faced by neurodivergent individuals.

The Power of ADHD

ADHD, in particular, brings its own strengths and contributions to neurodiversity:

1. **Creativity:** Many individuals with ADHD have a natural flair for creativity, thinking outside the box, and generating novel ideas.

2. **Hyperfocus:** While attention may be challenging in some situations, ADHD can also manifest as hyperfocus—a state of intense concentration and productivity on tasks of interest.

3. **Divergent Thinking:** ADHD often leads to divergent thinking, where connections are made between seemingly unrelated concepts, fostering innovation and problem-solving.

4. **Energetic Approach:** The energy and enthusiasm that accompany ADHD can be harnessed positively, driving passion, motivation, and drive in pursuits and projects.

Challenges and Misconceptions

Despite its strengths, ADHD also comes with challenges and misconceptions. Common misconceptions include the belief that ADHD is a result of poor parenting or a lack of intelligence. It's crucial to challenge these misconceptions and promote accurate understanding and support for individuals with ADHD.

Creating Neurodiverse Spaces

Creating neurodiverse-friendly spaces involves implementing strategies and practices that accommodate diverse cognitive styles and needs. This includes:

1. **Flexible Work Environments:** Providing flexibility in work schedules, tasks, and communication styles to accommodate neurodivergent employees.

2. **Sensory Considerations:** Creating sensory-friendly environments with options for noise reduction, comfortable seating, and visual supports.

3. **Clear Communication:** Using clear, concise language and visual aids to enhance understanding and communication for neurodiverse individuals.

4. **Accommodations and Supports:** Offering accommodations such as extra time on tasks, organizational tools, and support from trained professionals.

Advocacy and Awareness

Advocating for neurodiversity involves raising awareness, challenging stigma, and promoting inclusive practices in education, employment, healthcare, and communities. It requires ongoing efforts to educate the public, advocate for policy changes, and empower neurodivergent individuals to thrive in their chosen endeavors.

Conclusion

Embracing neurodiversity is not just about tolerance but about celebration, appreciation, and empowerment. By recognizing the power of ADHD and other neurodivergent traits, we can create a world where differences are valued, talents are nurtured, and everyone has the opportunity to contribute their unique gifts to society. This chapter invites you to embrace neurodiversity, celebrate differences, and unlock the full potential of a diverse and inclusive world.

CHAPTER 3

Leveraging Hyperfocus: Channeling Intense Focus for Productivity

Hyperfocus is a state of deep concentration and absorption in a task or activity that is of high interest or importance to an individual. In this chapter, we explore the concept of hyperfocus, its connection to ADHD, and strategies for harnessing this intense focus for enhanced productivity and achievement.

Understanding Hyperfocus

Hyperfocus is often seen as a paradox within ADHD—a condition characterized by difficulties in maintaining attention and focus, yet capable of intense concentration under the right circumstances. It is like a double-edged sword, capable of both hindering and facilitating productivity and achievement.

Hyperfocus and ADHD

Individuals with ADHD may experience hyperfocus as a spontaneous and involuntary shift in attention towards tasks or activities that captivate their interest or provide immediate gratification. This state of flow can lead to extended periods of focused work, high productivity, and a sense of accomplishment.

Benefits of Hyperfocus

Hyperfocus offers several benefits when effectively harnessed:

1. **Increased Productivity:** During hyperfocus, individuals can accomplish a significant amount of work in a relatively short time due to heightened concentration and reduced distractions.

2. **Quality of Work:** The intense focus of hyperfocus often results in high-quality outcomes as individuals immerse themselves deeply in the task at hand.

3. **Sense of Achievement:** Completing tasks during hyperfocus can boost self-esteem, motivation, and a sense of accomplishment, leading to a positive cycle of productivity.

4. **Time Perception:** In hyperfocus, time may seem to fly by, leading to a sense of time distortion where individuals may work longer than intended without feeling fatigued.

Identifying Triggers for Hyperfocus

Understanding what triggers hyperfocus is key to leveraging it effectively. Common triggers include:

1. **Interest and Passion:** Tasks or activities that align with an individual's interests, passions, or values are more likely to induce hyperfocus.

2. **Novelty and Challenge:** New or challenging tasks can capture attention and engage cognitive resources, leading to hyperfocus.

3. **Immediate Gratification:** Activities with immediate rewards or feedback, such as gaming or creative pursuits, can trigger hyperfocus.

4. **Deadline Pressure:** The pressure of impending deadlines can sometimes trigger hyperfocus as individuals focus intensely to meet the deadline.

Strategies for Harnessing Hyperfocus

While hyperfocus can be a valuable asset, it's essential to channel it effectively. Here are strategies for leveraging hyperfocus for productivity:

1. **Set Clear Goals:** Define specific, achievable goals for tasks to focus hyperfocus on desired outcomes.

2. **Manage Distractions:** Minimize external distractions and create a conducive environment for focused work.

3. **Time Blocking:** Allocate dedicated time blocks for tasks that benefit from hyperfocus, allowing for deep immersion without interruptions.

4. **Use Timers:** Set timers or alarms to remind yourself to take breaks and avoid burnout during hyperfocus sessions.

5. **Alternate Tasks:** Balance hyper-focused work with tasks that require less intense concentration to maintain overall productivity and prevent fatigue.

6. **Reflect and Evaluate:** After a hyperfocus session, reflect on your achievements, assess progress, and identify areas for improvement or adjustments.

Overcoming Challenges

While hyperfocus can be a powerful tool, it's essential to be mindful of potential challenges, such as:

1. **Tunnel Vision:** Hyperfocus can lead to tunnel vision, where individuals may overlook important details or neglect other responsibilities.

2. **Burnout:** Prolonged periods of hyperfocus without breaks can lead to mental and physical fatigue, impacting overall well-being.

3. **Neglecting Priorities:** In hyperfocus, individuals may prioritize tasks based on interest rather than importance, leading to neglect of essential responsibilities.

Balancing Hyperfocus and Flexibility

Finding a balance between hyperfocus and flexibility is key to sustainable productivity. Incorporating breaks, practicing mindfulness, and prioritizing self-care are essential for maintaining well-being while harnessing the benefits of hyperfocus.

Conclusion

Hyperfocus is a valuable asset for individuals with ADHD and anyone seeking to enhance productivity and achieve goals. By understanding its triggers, implementing effective strategies, and maintaining balance, hyperfocus can be channeled as a powerful tool for success. This chapter encourages you to embrace the intensity of hyperfocus, leverage its strengths, and unlock your potential for heightened productivity and accomplishment.

CHAPTER 4

Managing Distractions: Strategies for Maintaining Concentration

Distractions are a common challenge for individuals with ADHD and anyone navigating a fast-paced, information-rich world. In this chapter, we explore the nature of distractions, their impact on concentration, and practical strategies for managing distractions to maintain focus and productivity.

Understanding Distractions

Distractions come in various forms, from external stimuli like noise, interruptions, and digital notifications to internal distractions such as wandering thoughts, daydreaming, and impulsivity. They can disrupt focus, derail productivity, and contribute to feelings of overwhelm and frustration.

Impact of Distractions on Concentration

Distractions can have a significant impact on concentration and cognitive performance. They can lead to:

1. **Reduced Attention Span:** Constant distractions can shorten attention spans and make it challenging to sustain focus on tasks.

2. **Decreased Productivity:** Frequent interruptions and distractions can hinder productivity by disrupting workflow and task completion.

3. **Increased Errors:** Distractions can contribute to errors, mistakes, and oversight of important details, impacting the quality of work.

4. **Stress and Fatigue:** Managing distractions can lead to increased stress, mental fatigue, and a sense of being overwhelmed.

Types of Distractions

Distractions can be categorized into different types:

1. **External Distractions:** These include environmental factors like noise, visual clutter, interruptions from

colleagues or family members, and digital distractions such as social media notifications, emails, and phone calls.

2. **Internal Distractions:** Internal distractions stem from within, such as racing thoughts, daydreaming, worrying, or impulsivity that pulls attention away from the task at hand.

3. **Task-Related Distractions:** These distractions arise from multitasking, switching between tasks frequently, or feeling overwhelmed by the complexity of a task.

Strategies for Managing Distractions

Effective distraction management involves implementing strategies to minimize interruptions, maintain focus, and optimize productivity. Here are practical strategies for managing distractions:

1. **Create a Distraction-Free Environment:** Designate a quiet, organized workspace free from unnecessary stimuli and distractions. Use noise-canceling headphones, if needed, to block out background noise.

2. **Set Clear Boundaries:** Communicate boundaries to colleagues, family members, or roommates regarding

work hours, availability, and the importance of minimizing interruptions during focused work sessions.

3. **Digital Detox:** Limit digital distractions by turning off non-essential notifications, using website blockers or apps that promote focus, and scheduling specific times for checking emails and social media.

4. **Prioritize Tasks:** Use task prioritization techniques such as the Eisenhower Matrix or the Pomodoro Technique to focus on high-priority tasks while minimizing multitasking and task-switching.

5. **Mindfulness and Meditation:** Practice mindfulness and meditation to cultivate awareness of distractions, improve attentional control, and enhance the ability to refocus when distracted.

6. **Breaks and Movement:** Incorporate regular breaks and physical movement into your routine to refresh the mind, reduce mental fatigue, and improve overall focus and productivity.

7. **Organizational Tools:** Use organizational tools such as task lists, calendars, and productivity apps to stay organized, track progress, and manage deadlines effectively.

8. **Time Management Techniques:** Implement time-blocking, batching similar tasks together, and setting

realistic deadlines to create focused work periods and reduce the impact of distractions.

9. **Self-Reflection and Adjustment:** Reflect on patterns of distraction, identify triggers, and adjust strategies as needed to optimize concentration and productivity.

Overcoming Common Challenges

Managing distractions may encounter challenges such as:

1. **Internal Resistance:** Overcoming internal resistance to change habits, prioritize tasks, and maintain focus requires self-awareness, motivation, and persistence.

2. **External Interruptions:** Dealing with external interruptions may require assertiveness, clear communication, and boundary-setting skills to minimize disruptions.

3. **Technology Overload:** Balancing technology use and minimizing digital distractions requires mindful use of digital tools, setting boundaries, and prioritizing focused work periods.

Creating a Distraction-Resistant Mindset

Developing a distraction-resistant mindset involves cultivating habits, routines, and strategies that support sustained focus, resilience to distractions, and adaptive coping mechanisms when faced with challenges.

Conclusion

Over time, the ability to control distractions can be honed and improved. By implementing effective strategies, creating a conducive work environment, and cultivating a distraction-resistant mindset, you can enhance concentration, productivity, and overall well-being. This chapter encourages you to take proactive steps in managing distractions, reclaiming control over your attention, and optimizing your ability to stay focused and productive in a distracting world.

CHAPTER 5

Navigating Time Management: Tools for Organizing Your Day

Time management is a fundamental skill that plays a crucial role in productivity, efficiency, and overall well-being. In this chapter, we delve into the principles of effective time management and explore practical tools and strategies for organizing your day to maximize productivity and achieve your goals.

Understanding Time Management

Time management involves the process of planning, prioritizing, and allocating time to tasks and activities based on their importance, urgency, and impact. It's about making intentional choices about how you use your time to optimize productivity and achieve desired outcomes.

The Importance of Time Management

Effective time management offers numerous benefits:

1. **Increased Productivity:** Properly managed time leads to improved productivity, as tasks are completed efficiently and deadlines are met.

2. **Reduced Stress:** By organizing tasks and setting realistic timelines, time management helps reduce stress and prevent last-minute rushes.

3. **Improved Focus:** Prioritizing tasks and minimizing distractions enhances focus and concentration, leading to higher-quality work.

4. **Better Work-Life Balance:** Effective time management allows for better allocation of time between work, personal life, and leisure activities, promoting a healthier balance.

Principles of Effective Time Management

Effective time management is guided by several principles:

1. **Goal Setting:** Start by defining clear, specific goals and objectives to guide your priorities and actions.

2. **Prioritization:** Identify high-priority tasks and focus on completing them first, considering factors like deadlines, importance, and impact.

3. **Time Blocking:** Allocate dedicated time blocks for different tasks and activities, ensuring focused work periods and avoiding multitasking.

4. **Schedule Flexibility:** Allow for flexibility in your schedule to accommodate unexpected tasks, interruptions, and changes in priorities.

5. **Task Breakdown:** Break down larger tasks into smaller, manageable steps to prevent overwhelm and facilitate progress.

6. **Regular Review:** Regularly review your progress, adjust priorities as needed, and reflect on time management strategies for continuous improvement.

Tools for Time Management

Effective time management is aided by a variety of tools and methods, including:

1. **Calendar Apps:** Use digital calendar apps like Google Calendar, Outlook Calendar, or Apple Calendar to

schedule appointments, set reminders, and plan your day.

2. **Task Management Apps:** Utilize task management apps such as Todoist, Trello, or Asana to create task lists, set deadlines, track progress, and collaborate with others.

3. **Time Tracking Tools:** Use time tracking tools like Toggl, RescueTime, or Clockify to monitor how you spend your time, identify time wasters, and optimize productivity.

4. **Prioritization Methods:** Apply prioritization techniques such as the Eisenhower Matrix, ABC prioritization, or Pareto Principle (80/20 rule) to focus on tasks that yield the most significant results.

5. **Time Blocking:** Implement time blocking by scheduling specific time slots for different activities, including focused work, meetings, breaks, and personal tasks.

6. **Pomodoro Technique:** Use the Pomodoro Technique, a time management method involving work intervals (e.g., 25 minutes) followed by short breaks to maintain focus and productivity.

7. **Weekly and Daily Planning:** Set aside time each week and day for planning and organizing tasks, setting goals, and reviewing progress.

8. **Mindfulness Practices:** Incorporate mindfulness practices such as meditation, deep breathing, or mindfulness breaks to enhance focus, reduce stress, and improve overall well-being.

Overcoming Time Management Challenges

Common challenges in time management include procrastination, poor delegation, overcommitment, and ineffective prioritization. Overcoming these challenges requires self-awareness, discipline, and the willingness to adopt new habits and strategies.

Creating Your Time Management System

Designing a personalized time management system involves:

1. **Identifying Goals:** Clarify your short-term and long-term goals to align your time management efforts with your desired outcomes.

2. **Choosing Tools:** Select time management tools and techniques that resonate with your preferences, workflow, and organizational needs.

3. **Consistent Implementation:** Implement your time management system consistently, adjusting and refining it as needed based on feedback and results.

4. **Seeking Support:** Seek support from mentors, coaches, or peers who can provide guidance, accountability, and encouragement in your time management journey.

Conclusion

It is possible to acquire and improve effective time management skills over time. By understanding the principles of time management, leveraging tools and techniques, and addressing common challenges, you can organize your day more efficiently, optimize productivity, and achieve your goals with greater focus and effectiveness. This chapter encourages you to take proactive steps in managing your time, embracing productivity-enhancing strategies, and creating a balanced and fulfilling daily routine.

CHAPTER 6

Building Resilience: Overcoming Setbacks and Adversity

Resilience is the ability to bounce back from challenges, setbacks, and adversity. In this chapter, we explore the concept of resilience, its importance in navigating life's ups and downs, and strategies for developing and strengthening resilience in the face of obstacles.

Understanding Resilience

Resilience is not about avoiding difficulties but about adapting, learning, and growing stronger in the face of adversity. It involves psychological, emotional, and cognitive processes that enable individuals to maintain a sense of well-being, cope with stress, and persevere through tough times.

The Importance of Resilience

In many facets of life, resilience is essential:

1. **Coping with Challenges:** Resilience equips individuals with the tools and mindset to cope effectively with challenges, setbacks, and unexpected events.

2. **Promoting Mental Health:** Resilience contributes to positive mental health by fostering adaptive coping strategies, emotional regulation, and self-efficacy.

3. **Enhancing Performance:** Resilient individuals are better equipped to handle pressure, maintain focus, and perform well under stressful conditions.

4. **Building Relationships:** Resilience strengthens relationships by promoting empathy, communication skills, and the ability to navigate conflicts constructively.

5. **Supporting Growth:** Resilience fosters personal growth, self-awareness, and a sense of purpose, leading to increased confidence and motivation to pursue goals.

Characteristics of Resilient Individuals

Resilient individuals often exhibit the following characteristics:

1. **Optimism:** A positive outlook and belief in one's ability to overcome challenges.

2. **Adaptability:** Flexibility and openness to change, new perspectives, and alternative solutions.

3. **Problem-Solving Skills:** Effective problem-solving abilities and resourcefulness in finding solutions.

4. **Emotional Regulation:** The ability to manage emotions, cope with stress, and maintain emotional balance.

5. **Social Support:** Strong social connections, supportive relationships, and access to a network of resources and assistance.

6. **Self-Compassion:** Kindness and understanding toward oneself, even in the face of setbacks or failures.

7. **Resilience Mindset:** A mindset that views challenges as opportunities for growth, learning, and personal development.

Strategies for Building Resilience

Developing resilience involves intentional efforts and strategies:

1. **Cultivate Self-Awareness:** Increase self-awareness of your strengths, weaknesses, values, and coping mechanisms.

2. **Practice Mindfulness:** Incorporate mindfulness practices such as meditation, deep breathing, or mindfulness exercises to enhance awareness, reduce stress, and promote emotional balance.

3. **Build a Support Network:** Cultivate supportive relationships with friends, family, mentors, or support groups who can provide encouragement, guidance, and perspective during challenging times.

4. **Set Realistic Goals:** Break down larger goals into smaller, achievable steps, and celebrate progress along the way to maintain motivation and momentum.

5. **Develop Problem-Solving Skills:** Enhance problem-solving abilities by brainstorming solutions, seeking feedback, and learning from past experiences.

6. **Practice Self-Care:** Prioritize self-care activities such as adequate sleep, healthy eating, regular exercise, and relaxation techniques to support overall well-being.

7. **Maintain Perspective:** Foster a balanced perspective by reframing challenges as opportunities for learning, growth, and resilience-building.

8. **Seek Learning Opportunities:** Embrace opportunities for learning, skill development, and personal growth, even in difficult circumstances.

9. **Practice Gratitude:** Cultivate a practice of gratitude by focusing on positive aspects of life, expressing appreciation, and acknowledging achievements, no matter how small.

Overcoming Setbacks and Adversity

When facing setbacks and adversity, resilient individuals:

1. **Acknowledge Emotions:** Allow yourself to acknowledge and process emotions such as disappointment, frustration, or sadness in a healthy manner.

2. **Learn from Failure:** View failures as learning experiences, extract lessons and insights, and apply them to future endeavors.

3. **Seek Support:** Reach out for support from trusted individuals, seek professional guidance if needed, and leverage available resources and services.

4. **Practice Resilience-Building Activities:** Engage in activities that promote resilience, such as journaling, practicing gratitude, seeking new challenges, and maintaining a sense of humor.

5. **Stay Flexible:** Adapt to changing circumstances, adjust goals or strategies as needed, and remain open to alternative paths to success.

Conclusion

Building resilience is a lifelong journey that involves cultivating skills, adopting a resilient mindset, and leveraging support networks and resources. By developing resilience, you can navigate life's challenges with greater confidence, adaptability, and inner strength. This chapter encourages you to embrace resilience-building strategies, overcome setbacks and adversity, and thrive in the face of challenges, ultimately leading to personal growth, well-being, and success.

CHAPTER 7

Enhancing Communication: Strategies for Effective Interactions

Effective communication is essential for building relationships, fostering collaboration, and achieving mutual understanding. In this chapter, we explore the principles of effective communication and strategies for enhancing interpersonal interactions in various contexts.

Understanding Effective Communication

Effective communication involves the clear and meaningful exchange of information, ideas, thoughts, and feelings between individuals or groups. It encompasses verbal and nonverbal communication, active listening, empathy, clarity, and mutual respect.

The Importance of Effective Communication

Effective communication is vital for several reasons:

1. **Building Relationships:** Good communication strengthens relationships by promoting trust, transparency, and open dialogue.

2. **Conflict Resolution:** Effective communication skills are crucial for resolving conflicts, addressing misunderstandings, and finding mutually acceptable solutions.

3. **Team Collaboration:** In collaborative settings, effective communication fosters teamwork, coordination, and shared goals.

4. **Leadership:** Strong communication skills are essential for effective leadership, including clear direction, delegation, feedback, and motivation.

5. **Personal Development:** Enhancing communication skills contributes to personal growth, self-awareness, and improved relationships both professionally and personally.

Principles of Effective Communication

Effective communication is guided by several principles:

1. **Clarity:** Communicate clearly and concisely, using simple language and avoiding jargon or ambiguity.

2. **Active Listening:** Practice active listening by paying attention, paraphrasing, asking clarifying questions, and showing empathy.

3. **Nonverbal Cues:** Pay attention to nonverbal cues such as body language, facial expressions, tone of voice, and gestures, as they convey additional meaning.

4. **Empathy:** Empathize with others' perspectives, feelings, and experiences to foster understanding and connection.

5. **Respect:** Treat others with respect, courtesy, and professionalism, regardless of differences or disagreements.

6. **Feedback:** Provide constructive feedback that is specific, timely, and focused on behaviors or actions, not personal traits.

7. **Adaptability:** Be adaptable in your communication style, adjusting to the needs, preferences, and cultural backgrounds of others.

Strategies for Enhancing Communication

1. **Active Listening:** Practice active listening by giving full attention, maintaining eye contact, nodding, summarizing key points, and avoiding interruptions.

2. **Clarification:** Seek clarification when needed by asking open-ended questions, paraphrasing, and confirming understanding.

3. **Empathetic Communication:** Show empathy by acknowledging others' emotions, validating their experiences, and expressing understanding.

4. **Assertive Communication:** Be assertive in expressing your thoughts, opinions, and needs clearly and respectfully, while also listening to and considering others' perspectives.

5. **Nonverbal Communication:** Pay attention to your body language, facial expressions, tone of voice, and gestures to ensure they align with your intended message.

6. **Effective Feedback:** Provide constructive feedback using the "sandwich" approach—start with positive feedback, address areas for improvement, and end with encouragement or praise.

7. **Conflict Resolution:** Use effective communication skills to resolve conflicts by focusing on facts, active listening, finding common ground, and seeking win-win solutions.

8. **Cultural Awareness:** Be mindful of cultural differences in communication styles, norms, and expectations, adapting your approach to promote inclusivity and understanding.

9. **Digital Communication:** Apply effective communication principles to digital interactions, including email etiquette, clarity in written communication, and using appropriate tone and language.

Overcoming Communication Challenges

Common communication challenges include miscommunication, misunderstandings, cultural differences, emotional barriers, and conflicts. Overcoming these challenges requires:

1. **Self-Awareness:** Increase self-awareness of your communication style, biases, triggers, and areas for improvement.

2. **Active Learning:** Continuously seek opportunities to improve communication skills through training, practice, feedback, and reflection.

3. **Flexibility:** Be flexible and adaptable in your communication approach, considering the context, audience, and objectives of each interaction.

4. **Conflict Resolution Skills:** Develop skills for effective conflict resolution, including active listening, empathy, perspective-taking, and collaborative problem-solving.

5. **Seeking Feedback:** Solicit feedback from others on your communication style, seeking constructive criticism and areas for growth.

Conclusion

Enhancing communication is a lifelong journey that involves continuous learning, practice, and adaptation. By applying effective communication strategies, fostering empathy, active listening, and respectful dialogue, you can improve relationships, resolve conflicts, and achieve mutual understanding in various personal and professional settings.

This chapter encourages you to embrace effective communication skills, navigate communication challenges, and cultivate positive and meaningful interactions with others.

CHAPTER 8

Cultivating Relationships: Nurturing Connections in Personal and Professional Life

Relationships play a vital role in our personal and professional lives, contributing to our well-being, success, and sense of fulfillment. In this chapter, we explore the importance of cultivating relationships, strategies for nurturing connections, and fostering meaningful interactions in various spheres of life.

Understanding Relationship Building

Relationship building involves establishing, maintaining, and strengthening connections with others based on mutual trust, respect, and understanding. It encompasses both personal relationships with family, friends, and partners, as well as professional relationships with colleagues, clients, and mentors.

The Importance of Relationships

Strong relationships offer numerous benefits:

1. **Support System:** Relationships provide emotional support, encouragement, and a sense of belonging during challenging times.

2. **Networking:** Professional relationships contribute to networking opportunities, career advancement, and access to resources and opportunities.

3. **Collaboration:** Positive relationships foster collaboration, teamwork, and synergistic partnerships that lead to shared goals and mutual success.

4. **Mental Health:** Healthy relationships promote mental well-being, reduce stress, and contribute to overall life satisfaction.

5. **Personal Growth:** Meaningful relationships encourage personal growth, self-awareness, and learning through diverse perspectives and experiences.

Strategies for Nurturing Relationships

1. **Communication:** Foster open, honest, and transparent communication to build trust, clarity, and mutual understanding.

2. **Active Listening:** Practice active listening by paying attention, validating feelings, asking clarifying questions, and showing empathy.

3. **Empathy:** Cultivate empathy by considering others' perspectives, emotions, and experiences, and responding with compassion and understanding.

4. **Quality Time:** Prioritize quality time with loved ones, friends, or colleagues through meaningful conversations, shared activities, and genuine connections.

5. **Consistency:** Be consistent in your interactions, follow through on commitments, and show reliability and dependability in your relationships.

6. **Boundaries:** Establish healthy boundaries that respect your needs, values, and priorities while also respecting the boundaries of others.

7. **Conflict Resolution:** Develop effective conflict resolution skills by addressing issues promptly, focusing on solutions, and maintaining respect and civility.

8. **Express Appreciation:** Show gratitude and appreciation for others' contributions, support, and presence in your life through words, gestures, or acts of kindness.

9. **Flexibility:** Be flexible and adaptable in your relationships, accommodating differences, navigating changes, and seeking win-win solutions.

10. **Self-Care:** Prioritize self-care and well-being to ensure you can contribute positively to relationships and maintain a healthy balance.

Building Professional Relationships

1. **Networking:** Attend networking events, conferences, and industry gatherings to expand your professional network, build connections, and foster collaborations.

2. **Mentorship:** Seek mentorship opportunities and cultivate relationships with mentors or mentees who

can provide guidance, support, and professional development.

3. **Team Building:** Foster teamwork, camaraderie, and a positive work culture by promoting communication, collaboration, and mutual respect within teams.

4. **Client Relationships:** Build strong relationships with clients by understanding their needs, delivering value, maintaining open communication, and providing excellent customer service.

Nurturing Personal Relationships

1. **Family Time:** Dedicate quality time to spend with family members, engage in shared activities, and create meaningful memories together.

2. **Friendships:** Cultivate friendships based on mutual interests, support, and positive interactions, and prioritize maintaining and nurturing these connections.

3. **Romantic Relationships:** Invest time and effort in nurturing romantic relationships through communication, appreciation, intimacy, and mutual respect.

4. **Self-Reflection:** Reflect on your relationships, assess their strengths and areas for improvement, and take proactive steps to nurture and strengthen them.

Overcoming Relationship Challenges

Common challenges in relationships include communication barriers, conflicts, misunderstandings, and distance. Overcoming these challenges requires:

1. **Effective Communication:** Improve communication skills by practicing active listening, expressing thoughts and feelings clearly, and seeking feedback.

2. **Conflict Resolution:** Develop skills for resolving conflicts constructively, addressing underlying issues, and finding mutually acceptable solutions.

3. **Empathy:** Cultivate empathy by considering others' perspectives, validating emotions, and showing understanding and compassion.

4. **Boundaries:** Set and maintain healthy boundaries that promote mutual respect, trust, and balance in relationships.

5. **Continuous Improvement:** Commit to continuous improvement in relationships by seeking feedback, learning from experiences, and adapting strategies as needed.

Conclusion

Cultivating relationships is an ongoing process that requires effort, understanding, and investment of time and energy. By prioritizing effective communication, empathy, consistency, and self-care, you can nurture meaningful connections, foster trust, and build strong, supportive relationships in both your personal and professional life. This chapter encourages you to embrace relationship-building strategies, overcome challenges, and cultivate fulfilling connections that enrich your life and contribute to your overall well-being and success.

CHAPTER 9

Career Success with ADHD: Leveraging Strengths in the Workplace

Navigating the professional landscape with ADHD presents unique challenges and opportunities. In this chapter, we delve into strategies for leveraging strengths, overcoming obstacles, and achieving career success while embracing neurodiversity in the workplace.

Understanding ADHD in the Workplace

ADHD can impact various aspects of work, including attention, focus, organization, time management, and task completion. However, individuals with ADHD often possess strengths that can be valuable in the workplace, such as creativity, problem-solving abilities, hyperfocus, resilience, and adaptability.

Leveraging Strengths

1. **Creativity:** Harness your creativity to generate innovative ideas, think outside the box, and contribute unique perspectives to projects and teams.

2. **Problem-Solving Skills:** Use your problem-solving abilities to identify solutions, troubleshoot challenges, and find efficient ways to accomplish tasks.

3. **Hyperfocus:** Channel hyperfocus into tasks that require deep concentration and attention to detail, leading to high-quality outcomes and productivity.

4. **Resilience:** Draw upon your resilience to bounce back from setbacks, learn from failures, and maintain motivation and perseverance in the face of challenges.

5. **Adaptability:** Embrace your adaptability by quickly adjusting to changing priorities, environments, and demands, demonstrating flexibility and agility in your work approach.

Navigating Challenges

1. **Time Management:** Develop strategies for managing time effectively, such as prioritizing tasks, using

calendars and reminders, breaking tasks into smaller steps, and setting realistic deadlines.

2. **Organization:** Implement organizational tools and systems, such as task lists, project management software, and filing systems, to maintain order and structure in your work.

3. **Focus and Distractions:** Minimize distractions by creating a conducive work environment, using noise-canceling headphones, setting boundaries, and practicing mindfulness techniques.

4. **Communication:** Enhance communication skills by being clear, concise, and specific in your messages, actively listening to others, asking clarifying questions, and seeking feedback.

5. **Task Completion:** Break down tasks into manageable steps, set achievable goals, track progress, and celebrate milestones to stay motivated and focused on completing projects.

Advocating for Accommodations

If needed, advocate for accommodations in the workplace to support your productivity and well-being. Examples of accommodations for ADHD may include flexible work hours, noise-reducing equipment, ergonomic furniture, task prioritization assistance, and access to coaching or mentoring programs.

Building a Support Network

1. **Colleagues:** Build positive relationships with colleagues by being collaborative, respectful, and supportive, fostering a sense of teamwork and camaraderie.

2. **Mentors:** Seek guidance and mentorship from experienced professionals who can provide insights, advice, and career development support.

3. **ADHD Support Groups:** Connect with ADHD support groups or networks, both within and outside the workplace, to share experiences, resources, and strategies for success.

4. **Professional Development:** Invest in ongoing learning and skill development through workshops, courses, certifications, and networking events to enhance your expertise and career opportunities.

Embracing Neurodiversity

Promote neurodiversity awareness and inclusion in the workplace by advocating for diverse perspectives, accommodations, and support for neurodivergent individuals. Educate colleagues and employers about ADHD, its strengths, challenges, and the value of creating an inclusive work environment that celebrates diversity.

Seeking Career Growth

1. **Goal Setting:** Set clear career goals, both short-term and long-term, and develop action plans to achieve them, leveraging your strengths and addressing areas for growth.

2. **Professional Development:** Pursue opportunities for professional development, such as training programs, skill-building workshops, certifications, and advanced education, to enhance your expertise and marketability.

3. **Networking:** Expand your professional network through networking events, industry conferences, online platforms, and mentorship programs to explore new opportunities, gain insights, and build connections.

4. **Feedback and Reflection:** Seek feedback from supervisors, peers, and mentors, reflect on your strengths and areas for improvement, and use feedback constructively to enhance your performance and career trajectory.

5. **Career Transitions:** Consider potential career transitions or advancements that align with your interests, strengths, and long-term goals, exploring new roles, industries, or opportunities for growth and development.

Conclusion

Career success with ADHD is achievable by leveraging strengths, navigating challenges, advocating for accommodations and support, building relationships, embracing neurodiversity, and pursuing continuous learning and growth. This chapter encourages you to embrace your strengths, seek support and resources, advocate for inclusion and accommodations, and pursue meaningful and fulfilling career opportunities that align with your strengths, values, and aspirations. With resilience, determination, and a proactive approach, you can thrive in your career and make valuable contributions in the workplace.

CHAPTER 10

Self-Care and Wellness: Prioritizing Mental and Physical Health

In the pursuit of a fulfilling life, prioritizing self-care and wellness is paramount. This chapter explores strategies for maintaining mental and physical health, managing stress, and fostering overall well-being in the context of a busy and dynamic lifestyle.

Understanding Self-Care and Wellness

Activities and practices that support one's physical, mental, and emotional well-being are included in self-care. It involves taking intentional steps to nurture oneself, manage stress, and maintain a healthy balance in life. Wellness, on the other hand, encompasses holistic well-being across various dimensions, including physical, emotional, social, intellectual, occupational, and spiritual aspects.

Importance of Self-Care and Wellness

Prioritizing self-care and wellness offers numerous benefits:

1. **Improved Mental Health:** Self-care practices contribute to reduced stress, anxiety, and depression, leading to improved mental health and emotional resilience.

2. **Enhanced Physical Health:** Wellness activities such as exercise, nutrition, and adequate sleep support physical health, energy levels, and overall vitality.

3. **Stress Management:** Self-care strategies help manage stress, prevent burnout, and promote relaxation, rejuvenation, and balance.

4. **Increased Productivity:** Prioritizing self-care leads to increased productivity, focus, creativity, and effectiveness in personal and professional endeavors.

5. **Better Relationships:** Self-care fosters healthier relationships by promoting self-awareness, emotional regulation, and the ability to support and connect with others.

Strategies for Self-Care and Wellness

1. **Physical Health:** Prioritize regular physical activity, balanced nutrition, adequate sleep, and regular health check-ups to support overall physical well-being.

2. **Mental Health:** Practice mindfulness, meditation, relaxation techniques, and seek professional support if needed to manage stress, anxiety, and other mental health concerns.

3. **Emotional Well-being:** Cultivate self-awareness, emotional intelligence, positive self-talk, and healthy coping mechanisms to nurture emotional resilience and well-being.

4. **Social Connections:** Maintain supportive relationships, engage in social activities, seek social support, and foster connections that contribute to a sense of belonging and fulfillment.

5. **Intellectual Stimulation:** Engage in lifelong learning, pursue hobbies and interests, challenge yourself intellectually, and seek opportunities for growth and development.

6. **Work-Life Balance:** Establish boundaries between work and personal life, prioritize leisure activities, hobbies, and downtime to recharge and prevent burnout.

7. **Time Management:** Manage time effectively, delegate tasks when possible, set realistic goals and priorities, and practice time management strategies to reduce stress and enhance productivity.

8. **Healthy Habits:** Develop healthy habits such as regular exercise, nutritious eating, hydration, proper hygiene, and avoiding harmful substances to support overall well-being.

9. **Mind-Body Practices:** Incorporate mind-body practices such as yoga, tai chi, qigong, or breathwork to promote relaxation, stress reduction, and mind-body harmony.

10. **Nature and Outdoor Time:** Spend time in nature, engage in outdoor activities, and connect with natural surroundings to boost mood, reduce stress, and enhance well-being.

Stress Management

1. **Identify Stressors:** Identify sources of stress in your life, both personal and professional, and explore strategies to manage or minimize their impact.

2. **Stress Reduction Techniques:** Practice stress reduction techniques such as deep breathing, progressive muscle relaxation, visualization, or journaling to promote relaxation and calmness.

3. **Time Management:** Use time management techniques, prioritize tasks, set boundaries, and delegate responsibilities to reduce overwhelm and stress.

4. **Self-Compassion:** Be kind and compassionate toward yourself, practice self-care, and avoid self-criticism or perfectionism that can contribute to stress.

5. **Seek Support:** Reach out for support from friends, family, colleagues, or mental health professionals if stress becomes overwhelming or affects your well-being.

Creating a Self-Care Plan

Develop a personalized self-care plan that incorporates activities, practices, and strategies that support your physical, mental, and emotional well-being. Consider factors such as your preferences, interests, lifestyle, and specific areas of focus for self-care.

Maintaining Consistency

Consistency is key to effective self-care and wellness. Create daily, weekly, and monthly routines that prioritize self-care activities, establish healthy habits, and ensure ongoing maintenance of your well-being.

Overcoming Barriers to Self-Care

Identify and address barriers to self-care, such as time constraints, competing priorities, perfectionism, guilt, or lack of resources. Adopt a proactive approach to overcoming obstacles and making self-care a priority in your life.

Conclusion

Prioritizing self-care and wellness are an essential investment in your overall well-being, happiness, and quality of life. By incorporating self-care practices, stress management techniques, healthy habits, and a holistic approach to well-being, you can nurture your physical, mental, and emotional health, enhance resilience, and thrive in all areas of your life. This chapter encourages you to embrace self-care as a lifelong journey, adapt strategies to your unique needs and preferences, and prioritize your well-being as a foundation for success, fulfillment, and happiness.

CHAPTER 11

Overcoming Procrastination: Techniques for Getting Things Done

Procrastination is a common challenge that can hinder productivity, increase stress, and create barriers to achieving goals. In this chapter, we explore strategies and techniques for overcoming procrastination, improving time management, and increasing productivity.

Understanding Procrastination

Procrastination is the act of delaying or postponing tasks or activities, often due to avoidance, fear, lack of motivation, or perfectionism. It can lead to feelings of guilt, anxiety, and frustration, as well as decreased productivity and progress toward goals.

The Impact of Procrastination

Procrastination can have various negative effects:

1. **Reduced Productivity:** Procrastination causes delays in finishing assignments, which lowers efficiency and productivity all around.

2. **Increased Stress:** Procrastination contributes to increased stress, anxiety, and pressure as deadlines approach.

3. **Missed Opportunities:** Procrastination can result in missed opportunities, overlooked priorities, and unfulfilled goals.

4. **Job Quality:** Procrastination can lead to rushing through tasks, which can lower job quality and thoroughness.

5. **Self-Perception:** Procrastination can affect self-esteem, confidence, and motivation, leading to a cycle of procrastination and negative self-talk.

Strategies for Overcoming Procrastination

1. **Set Clear Goals:** Define clear, specific, and achievable goals to provide direction and motivation for tasks and projects.

2. **Break Tasks into Smaller Steps:** Break down larger tasks into smaller, manageable steps to reduce overwhelm and increase motivation.

3. **Prioritize Tasks:** Use prioritization techniques such as the Eisenhower Matrix or ABC prioritization to focus on high-priority tasks and activities.

4. **Create a Schedule:** Develop a schedule or timetable for tasks, allocating specific time blocks for focused work, breaks, and relaxation.

5. **Set Deadlines:** Establish realistic deadlines for tasks to create a sense of urgency and accountability.

6. **Use Time Blocking:** Allocate dedicated time blocks for different tasks and activities, avoiding multitasking and distractions.

7. **Eliminate Distractions:** Minimize distractions by creating a conducive work environment, turning off notifications, and using focus techniques such as the Pomodoro Technique.

8. **Practice Self-Discipline:** Develop self-discipline and self-control by setting boundaries, avoiding procrastination triggers, and staying focused on priorities.

9. **Reward Progress:** Reward yourself for completing tasks or making progress toward goals, using incentives to motivate and reinforce positive behavior.

10. **Visualize Success:** Use visualization techniques to imagine yourself completing tasks successfully and experiencing the benefits of productivity and achievement.

11. **Seek Accountability:** Share your goals and progress with others, such as friends, colleagues, or mentors, to gain accountability and support.

12. **Address Perfectionism:** Recognize perfectionism as a barrier to productivity, focus on progress over perfection, and embrace a growth mindset that values learning and improvement.

13. **Practice Self-Compassion:** Be kind and compassionate toward yourself, acknowledging that setbacks and mistakes are part of the learning process.

Overcoming Procrastination Challenges

1. **Identify Procrastination Triggers:** Identify factors that contribute to procrastination, such as fear of failure, lack of confidence, boredom, or perfectionism.

2. **Challenge Negative Thoughts:** Challenge negative thoughts and beliefs that contribute to procrastination, replacing them with more positive and empowering perspectives.

3. **Develop Coping Strategies:** Develop coping strategies for managing stress, anxiety, and overwhelm, such as mindfulness, relaxation techniques, or physical activity.

4. **Seek Support:** Reach out for support from friends, family, colleagues, or mental health professionals if procrastination becomes a persistent challenge affecting your well-being and productivity.

Creating a Procrastination Action Plan

Create a personalized action plan for overcoming procrastination, incorporating specific strategies, techniques, and accountability measures to address procrastination challenges effectively.

Conclusion

Overcoming procrastination requires self-awareness, motivation, discipline, and effective strategies for managing time, priorities, and mindset. By implementing proactive techniques, setting clear goals, managing distractions, and seeking support when needed, you can break free from procrastination habits, increase productivity, and achieve greater success and fulfillment in your personal and professional life. This chapter encourages you to take proactive steps, develop resilience, and cultivate habits that support productivity, focus, and progress toward your goals.

CHAPTER 12

Financial Management: Budgeting and Planning for Long-Term Goals

Financial management is a crucial aspect of life that involves budgeting, saving, investing, and planning for long-term financial security and goals. In this chapter, we'll explore strategies and techniques for effective financial management, including budgeting, saving, debt management, and planning for long-term financial objectives.

Understanding Financial Management

Financial management refers to the process of planning, organizing, controlling, and monitoring financial resources to achieve financial goals and objectives. It involves making informed decisions about income, expenses, savings, investments, and debt management to ensure financial stability, security, and growth.

The Importance of Financial Management

Effective financial management offers several benefits:

1. **Financial Stability:** Financial management helps maintain stability by ensuring income covers expenses, emergencies are prepared for, and debt is managed responsibly.

2. **Goal Achievement:** Financial management enables individuals to set and achieve financial goals, such as homeownership, retirement savings, education funding, or travel plans.

3. **Debt Reduction:** Proper financial management strategies help reduce and manage debt, avoiding excessive interest payments and improving financial health.

4. **Investment Growth:** Financial management includes investment planning to grow wealth over time, build retirement funds, and achieve long-term financial security.

5. **Emergency Preparedness:** Financial management involves creating emergency funds and contingency plans to handle unexpected expenses or income disruptions.

Strategies for Effective Financial Management

1. **Budgeting:** Create a detailed budget that outlines income, expenses, savings goals, and debt repayment plans. Use budgeting tools or apps to track expenses and monitor progress.

2. **Savings Goals:** Set specific savings goals for short-term needs (e.g., emergency fund, vacation fund) and long-term goals (e.g., retirement savings, major purchases).

3. **Debt Management:** Develop a plan to manage and reduce debt, focusing on high-interest debts first and exploring strategies such as debt consolidation or negotiation with creditors.

4. **Investment Planning:** Determine investment strategies based on risk tolerance, financial goals, and time horizon. Consider diversified investment portfolios, retirement accounts (e.g., 401(k), IRA), and professional financial advice.

5. **Insurance Coverage:** Review insurance needs, including health insurance, life insurance, disability insurance, and property insurance, to protect against unforeseen risks and liabilities.

6. **Estate Planning:** Create an estate plan that includes wills, trusts, power of attorney documents, and healthcare directives to manage assets and ensure wishes are carried out.

7. **Tax Planning:** Implement tax planning strategies to minimize tax liabilities, take advantage of tax deductions and credits, and optimize tax-efficient investments.

8. **Financial Education:** Continuously educate yourself about personal finance topics, investment options, tax laws, and financial planning strategies to make informed decisions.

Budgeting Basics

1. **Income:** Identify all sources of income, including salary, bonuses, freelance work, investments, and other sources.

2. **Expenses:** List all monthly expenses, including fixed expenses (e.g., rent/mortgage, utilities, insurance) and

variable expenses (e.g., groceries, entertainment, dining out).

3. **Savings Goals:** Allocate a portion of income toward savings goals, such as emergency funds, retirement savings, education funds, or specific financial goals.

4. **Debt Repayment:** Allocate funds toward debt repayment, focusing on high-interest debts first while maintaining minimum payments on other debts.

5. **Tracking and Adjusting:** Track expenses regularly, compare actual spending to budgeted amounts, and adjust as needed to stay on track with financial goals.

Saving and Investing

1. **Emergency Fund:** Build an emergency fund with 3-6 months' worth of living expenses to cover unexpected expenses or income disruptions.

2. **Retirement Savings:** Contribute to retirement accounts such as 401(k), IRA, or Roth IRA, taking advantage of employer matching contributions and tax benefits.

3. **Investment Diversification:** Diversify investment portfolios across asset classes (e.g., stocks, bonds, real estate) to reduce risk and maximize potential returns.

4. **Long-Term Goals:** Save and invest for long-term goals such as homeownership, education funding, travel plans, or starting a business, using appropriate investment vehicles and strategies.

Debt Management

1. **Debt Assessment:** Assess all debts, including credit cards, loans, and mortgages, noting interest rates, monthly payments, and total outstanding balances.

2. **Debt Repayment Plan:** Develop a debt repayment plan, prioritizing high-interest debts first while maintaining minimum payments on other debts.

3. **Debt Consolidation:** Explore options for debt consolidation or refinancing to lower interest rates, consolidate multiple debts into one payment, and simplify debt management.

4. **Negotiation:** Consider negotiating with creditors for lower interest rates, reduced payment plans, or debt settlement options if struggling to meet debt obligations.

Long-Term Financial Planning

1. **Retirement Planning:** Set retirement goals, estimate retirement expenses, and develop a retirement savings plan using retirement accounts, investments, and retirement calculators.

2. **Education Funding:** Plan for education expenses for yourself or family members, such as college savings plans (e.g., 529 plans), education savings accounts (e.g., Coverdell ESA), or other funding sources.

3. **Homeownership:** Save for a down payment, research mortgage options, and plan for homeownership costs such as property taxes, insurance, and maintenance.

4. **Estate Planning:** Create an estate plan that includes wills, trusts, beneficiary designations, and healthcare directives to manage assets and ensure wishes are carried out.

Financial Wellness and Mindset

1. **Financial Education:** Continuously educate yourself about personal finance topics, investment options, tax laws, and financial planning strategies to make informed decisions

2. **Financial Mindset:** Adopt a positive financial mindset focused on financial responsibility, long-term planning, disciplined spending, and goal achievement.

3. **Financial Goals:** Set SMART (Specific, Measurable, Achievable, Relevant, Time-bound) financial goals and regularly review progress, making adjustments as needed.

4. **Financial Health Checkups:** Conduct regular financial health checkups to assess progress toward goals, review budgets, track investments, and update financial plans as life circumstances change.

Conclusion

Effective financial management requires discipline, planning, education, and ongoing monitoring of financial goals and strategies. By implementing budgeting techniques, saving strategies, debt management plans, investment strategies, and long-term financial planning, you can achieve financial stability, security, and success in pursuing your financial goals and dreams. This chapter encourages you to take proactive steps, seek professional financial advice when needed, and prioritize financial wellness as an essential aspect of your overall well-being and life satisfaction.

CHAPTER 13

Creative Expression: Unleashing Artistic and Innovative Potential

Creative expression is a powerful tool for self-discovery, personal growth, and innovation. In this chapter, we explore the benefits of creative expression, techniques for nurturing creativity, and strategies for unleashing artistic and innovative potential in various aspects of life.

Understanding Creative Expression

Creative expression involves the exploration and communication of ideas, emotions, and perspectives through various artistic mediums, such as visual arts, writing, music, dance, theater, design, and more. It allows individuals to tap into their imagination, intuition, and unique talents to create something new, meaningful, and impactful.

The Benefits of Creative Expression

Engaging in creative expression offers numerous benefits:

1. **Self-Discovery:** Creative expression encourages self-discovery, introspection, and exploration of personal thoughts, feelings, and beliefs.

2. **Stress Reduction:** Immersing in creative activities can reduce stress, anxiety, and tension by providing a mindful, immersive, and enjoyable experience.

3. **Emotional Release:** Creative expression serves as an outlet for emotions, allowing individuals to express, process, and release pent-up feelings.

4. **Problem-Solving:** Creativity fosters innovative thinking, problem-solving skills, and the ability to generate new ideas, solutions, and perspectives.

5. **Self-Confidence:** Successfully creating and sharing creative work boosts self-confidence, self-esteem, and a sense of accomplishment.

6. **Communication:** Creative expression enhances communication skills, empathy, and the ability to

connect with others through shared experiences and emotions.

Techniques for Nurturing Creativity

1. **Mindfulness:** Practice mindfulness techniques such as meditation, deep breathing, or mindful observation to quiet the mind, enhance focus, and stimulate creativity.

2. **Playfulness:** Embrace a playful mindset, curiosity, and openness to experimentation, allowing yourself to explore without judgment or fear of failure.

3. **Diverse Experiences:** Seek diverse experiences, environments, cultures, and perspectives to inspire creativity, expand horizons, and spark new ideas.

4. **Inspiration:** Surround yourself with sources of inspiration, including books, art, music, nature, people, and experiences that ignite your imagination and creativity.

5. **Collaboration:** Collaborate with others, share ideas, seek feedback, and engage in creative dialogue and exchange to fuel creativity and innovation.

6. **Mind Mapping:** Use mind mapping techniques to visually organize ideas, connections, and possibilities, stimulating creative thinking and problem-solving.

7. **Creative Exercises:** Practice creative exercises such as brainstorming, freewriting, drawing, improvisation, or storytelling to stimulate creativity and generate ideas.

8. **Breaks and Reflection:** Take breaks, step away from tasks, and allow time for reflection and incubation of ideas, returning with fresh perspectives and insights.

9. **Challenge Assumptions:** Question assumptions, conventional wisdom, and established norms, encouraging unconventional thinking and creative breakthroughs.

10. **Risk-Taking:** Embrace risk-taking and experimentation, stepping outside comfort zones, and embracing failures as opportunities for learning and growth.

Unleashing Artistic and Innovative Potential

1. **Explore Different Mediums:** Experiment with different artistic mediums such as painting, drawing, writing, music, dance, photography, sculpture, digital art, or crafts to discover your strengths and preferences.

2. **Set Creative Goals:** Set specific creative goals, projects, or challenges to focus your creative energy and motivation, tracking progress and celebrating achievements.

3. **Create a Creative Space:** Designate a dedicated space for creative work, free from distractions, where you can immerse yourself in creative activities comfortably.

4. **Seek Feedback and Collaboration:** Share your creative work with others, seek constructive feedback, collaborate with fellow creators, and engage in creative communities or groups for inspiration and support.

5. **Embrace Imperfection:** Embrace imperfection, mistakes, and failures as part of the creative process, learning from setbacks and using them to fuel continued growth and innovation.

6. **Find Balance:** Balance creative pursuits with self-care, rest, and relaxation, avoiding burnout and maintaining a sustainable creative practice.

7. **Share Your Creativity:** Share your creative work with others through exhibitions, performances, publications, online platforms, or social media, connecting with audiences and receiving valuable feedback and recognition.

Applications of Creative Expression

1. **Personal Growth:** Use creative expression for personal growth, self-discovery, and emotional well-being, exploring themes, experiences, and ideas that resonate with you.

2. **Professional Development:** Apply creative expression in professional settings for problem-solving, innovation, communication, storytelling, branding, design, and leadership.

3. **Community Engagement:** Use creative expression to engage with communities, advocate for social causes, raise awareness, promote dialogue, and inspire positive change.

4. **Entrepreneurship:** Harness creative expression in entrepreneurship for product development, marketing, branding, customer engagement, and innovative business solutions.

Overcoming Creative Blocks

1. **Identify Blockages:** Identify and acknowledge creative blocks, such as fear, perfectionism, self-doubt, or lack

of inspiration, and explore strategies to overcome them.

2. **Break Routines:** Break out of creative routines or habits that stifle creativity, introducing novelty, variety, and new experiences to stimulate fresh ideas.

3. **Mindset Shift:** Adopt a growth mindset that embraces challenges, failures, and learning opportunities, reframing setbacks as stepping stones to creative growth.

4. **Collaborative Inspiration:** Collaborate with others, engage in creative workshops, classes, or brainstorming sessions to gain new perspectives, ideas, and inspiration.

5. **Self-Compassion:** Practice self-compassion and self-care during creative processes, nurturing a supportive and encouraging inner dialogue that fosters creativity and resilience.

6. **Creative Play:** Engage in creative play, exploration, and experimentation without attachment to outcomes, allowing freedom and spontaneity in creative expression.

Conclusion

Creative expression is a powerful vehicle for self-expression, innovation, problem solving, and personal growth. By nurturing creativity, exploring diverse artistic mediums, setting creative goals, seeking inspiration, collaborating with others, and overcoming creative blocks, you can unleash your artistic and innovative potential, enriching your life and contributing positively to the world around you.

CHAPTER 14

ADHD Across the Lifespan: Strategies for Children, Teens, and Adults

A neurodevelopmental disorder that affects people of all ages is attention-deficit/hyperactivity disorder, or ADHD. This chapter explores strategies tailored to children, teens, and adults with ADHD, focusing on managing symptoms, enhancing strengths, and promoting success in various life stages.

Understanding ADHD Across the Lifespan

ADHD manifests differently at different stages of life, presenting unique challenges and opportunities for growth. Understanding how ADHD impacts children, teens, and adults is essential for implementing effective strategies and support systems.

1. **Children:** ADHD in children often manifests as hyperactivity, impulsivity, inattention, and difficulties with organization, time management, and academic performance.

2. **Teens:** Adolescents with ADHD may face additional challenges such as academic demands, social relationships, self-esteem issues, time management, and executive function skills development.

3. **Adults:** Adults with ADHD may experience challenges in areas such as time management, organization, attention, impulsivity, emotional regulation, relationships, career success, and overall well-being.

Strategies for Children with ADHD

1. **Structured Routine:** Establish a structured daily routine with consistent schedules for activities, homework, meals, bedtime, and playtime to provide predictability and stability.

2. **Clear Expectations:** Set clear, age-appropriate expectations and guidelines for behavior, chores, responsibilities, and academic tasks, providing visual cues and reminders when needed.

3. **Positive Reinforcement:** Use positive reinforcement techniques such as praise, rewards, and incentives to reinforce desired behaviors, effort, and achievements.

4. **Break Tasks Into Steps:** Break down tasks into manageable steps, provide instructions in a clear and concise manner, and offer support and guidance as needed.

5. **Organizational Strategies:** Teach organizational skills such as using planners, checklists, color-coding, labeling, and organizing study materials to enhance organization and time management.

6. **Physical Activity:** Encourage regular physical activity and movement breaks to help channel excess energy and improve focus and attention.

7. **Social Skills Training:** Provide opportunities for social skills training, peer interactions, communication practice, and conflict resolution skills development.

8. **Educational Support:** Collaborate with teachers and educational professionals to implement accommodations, modifications, and support services such as specialized instruction, tutoring, or individualized education plans (IEPs).

Strategies for Teens with ADHD

1. **Executive Function Skills:** Teach executive function skills such as planning, organization, time management, prioritization, goal-setting, and self-monitoring.

2. **Study Strategies:** Provide study strategies and techniques such as breaking tasks into smaller chunks, using mnemonic devices, creating study guides, and practicing active learning.

3. **Self-Advocacy:** Encourage teens to advocate for themselves by communicating their needs, requesting accommodations, seeking support, and participating in decision-making regarding their education and well-being.

4. **Emotional Regulation:** Teach coping strategies for managing emotions, stress, and frustration, such as deep breathing, mindfulness, relaxation techniques, and problem-solving skills.

5. **Career Exploration:** Support teens in exploring interests, strengths, and career options, providing guidance, resources, and opportunities for skill development and career planning.

Strategies for Adults with ADHD

1. **Time Management:** Develop time management strategies such as using calendars, planners, reminders, and prioritizing tasks to improve productivity and organization.

2. **Organization Systems:** Implement organizational systems at home and work, such as decluttering, creating designated spaces, using digital tools, and establishing routines.

3. **Task Prioritization:** Prioritize tasks based on importance, deadlines, and energy levels, focusing on one task at a time and breaking larger projects into manageable steps.

4. **Distraction Management:** Minimize distractions by creating a conducive work environment, using time-blocking techniques, setting boundaries, and limiting multitasking.

5. **Self-Care:** Prioritize self-care practices such as regular exercise, adequate sleep, healthy nutrition, stress management, and relaxation techniques to support overall well-being.

6. **Career Strategies:** Identify strengths, interests, and career goals, seeking roles that align with strengths,

providing challenges, opportunities for growth, and accommodations if needed.

7. **Relationships:** Communicate openly with partners, family members, and friends about ADHD, educate them about symptoms and strategies, and collaborate on effective communication, support, and understanding.

Lifelong Strategies for ADHD Management

1. **Medication Management:** Work with healthcare professionals to explore medication options, dosage adjustments, and monitoring for effectiveness and side effects.

2. **Therapeutic Support:** Consider therapy or counseling for ADHD management, addressing challenges such as self-esteem, stress, emotional regulation, relationships, and coping strategies.

3. **Support Networks:** Build a support network of peers, family, friends, support groups, and professionals who understand ADHD and can provide encouragement, advice, and understanding.

4. **Continued Learning:** Stay informed about ADHD, research, treatments, and strategies for management through books, articles, workshops, and professional resources.

5. **Adaptive Strategies:** Develop adaptive strategies and tools such as apps, timers, alarms, reminders, and organizational aids to support daily functioning and ADHD management.

Conclusion

ADHD management across the lifespan requires a holistic approach that considers individual strengths, challenges, developmental stages, and needs. By implementing tailored strategies, seeking support, fostering self-awareness, and advocating for accommodations and understanding, individuals with ADHD can thrive academically, professionally, and personally. This chapter encourages a proactive approach to ADHD management, embracing strengths, addressing challenges, promoting self-advocacy, and fostering a supportive environment conducive to success and well-being across the lifespan.

CHAPTER 15

Building a Support Network: Finding Community and Resources

Building a strong support network is essential for individuals facing challenges such as ADHD, mental health concerns, or any other life circumstances. This chapter focuses on strategies for finding community, accessing resources, and cultivating a supportive network to enhance well-being and navigate life's complexities.

Understanding the Importance of a Support Network

A support network consists of individuals, organizations, and resources that provide emotional, practical, and informational support during challenging times. It offers a sense of belonging, understanding, validation, and encouragement, contributing to resilience, coping skills, and overall well-being.

Strategies for Building a Support Network

1. **Identify Supportive Individuals:** Identify friends, family members, colleagues, mentors, or peers who are understanding, empathetic, and supportive of your needs and challenges.

2. **Join Support Groups:** Seek out support groups, online communities, forums, or local organizations focused on ADHD, mental health, or specific interests where you can connect with others facing similar experiences.

3. **Professional Support:** Consult mental health professionals, therapists, counselors, coaches, or support services specializing in ADHD management, counseling, and therapeutic interventions.

4. **Community Resources:** Explore community resources such as clinics, support centers, advocacy organizations, hotlines, and educational programs offering information, support, and services related to ADHD and mental health.

5. **Online Platforms:** Utilize online platforms, social media groups, blogs, podcasts, and webinars dedicated

to ADHD awareness, education, advocacy, and peer support.

6. **Educational Workshops:** Attend workshops, seminars, conferences, or training sessions focused on ADHD management, coping strategies, skills development, and self-advocacy.

7. **Volunteer and Engage:** Get involved in volunteer activities, advocacy efforts, awareness campaigns, or community initiatives related to ADHD, mental health, or areas of interest, fostering connections and contributing to positive change.

8. **Build Meaningful Relationships:** Cultivate meaningful relationships based on mutual respect, trust, empathy, and shared experiences, nurturing supportive connections that offer encouragement, advice, and understanding.

Utilizing Your Support Network

1. **Open Communication:** Communicate openly and honestly with your support network about your needs, challenges, experiences, and goals, seeking feedback, advice, and validation.

2. **Seek Guidance:** Seek guidance, information, and resources from your support network, leveraging their

expertise, experiences, and perspectives to inform decision-making and problem-solving.

3. **Share Experiences:** Share your experiences, successes, setbacks, and insights with your support network, contributing to mutual learning, growth, and understanding.

4. **Offer Support:** Offer support, encouragement, and empathy to others in your support network facing challenges, providing a listening ear, validation, and practical assistance when needed.

5. **Celebrate Progress:** Celebrate progress, milestones, and achievements with your support network, recognizing and appreciating growth, resilience, and perseverance.

6. **Regular Check-Ins:** Maintain regular check-ins and communication with your support network, staying connected, informed, and engaged in ongoing support and collaboration.

Thank You Note

Thank you for embarking on this journey of exploration and learning. Building a support network is a powerful tool for navigating life's challenges, embracing growth, and fostering resilience. Always remember that asking for help is a sign of strength rather than weakness. Your support network is there to lift you up, provide guidance, and walk alongside you on your journey toward well-being and success.

Final Advice for the Reader

As you continue your journey, remember to be kind to yourself, practice self-care, and embrace both your strengths and challenges. Each step you take, each effort you make toward building a supportive community and accessing resources, is a meaningful investment in your well-being and personal growth. Keep learning, stay connected, and believe in your ability to thrive. You are not alone, and your journey is worth every step.

www.ingramcontent.com/pod-product-compliance
Lightning Source LLC
Chambersburg PA
CBHW050803250726

48653CB00006B/2052